A Prayer Journal for Baptism in the Holy Spirit

Therese Boucher

"I will ask the Father, and he will give you another Helper,
who will stay with you forever."
John 14:16

National Service Committee
Chariscenter USA
Box 628
Locust Grove, VA 22508-0628

Nihil Obstat: Rev. Joseph N. Rosie
Censor Librorum
Imprimatur: ✠ John M. Smith
Bishop of Trenton
April 3, 2003

The *Nihil Obstat* and the *Imprimatur* are official declarations
that a book or pamphlet is free of doctrinal or moral error. No
implication is contained therein that those who have granted
the *Nihil Obstat* or *Imprimatur* agree with the contents, opinions
or statements expressed.

Cover: *Living Breath* by Therese Boucher, design by
John Murello

ISBN 0-9677377-2-9

Contents

Introduction

Oct 24, 1998: Lois participated in a *Life in the Spirit Seminar*. Here is something she wrote in her journal after the first night:

> *God, I want more out of life. But what does more really mean? Help me find answers to this question. Help me open my heart and hear your voice. I place myself in your hands.*

June 3, 1895: St. Frances Cabrini wrote in her travel journal on a ship in the Gulf of Mexico.

> *The Holy Spirit is a sun whose light is reflected in just souls, a bottomless, shoreless ocean whose waters are beautiful, transparent, crystalline and life-giving, and flow continually and abundantly over souls who… do not oppose the Paraclete.*

Journals give voice to all kinds of adventures. Journals are for pioneers, travelers, spiritual pilgrims, sea captains, and soldiers gone to war. When journals describe the adventures of the heart they also point towards the greatest journey of all, the inner quest for love, for meaning and for new life with a capital "L".

Keeping a journal is a way of stopping beside the road and listening to yourself and to God. We are all pilgrims on a life-long journey that began before each of us was born. We travel in many different directions, but never alone. Jesus wants to be a life-long companion who points us toward the Father. He gives us the Holy Spirit as an inner guide. The Holy Spirit offers an unlimited supply of spiritual maps and signs for each leg of our spiritual journey.

This prayer journal is designed to help you search for your spiritual roots. You can explore what happens to you through the Sacraments of Initiation: Baptism, Confirmation and Eucharist. It doesn't matter what kinds of experiences you have had. God has immersed, or "baptized" you into the life of the Father, the Son and the Holy Spirit. You have a refreshing spring of leaping, life-giving water at the very core of your being. Finding this water and quenching your thirst will bring a new Pentecost, a new baptism in the Holy Spirit. You are created for new life in the Holy Spirit like a fish is made for life in the ocean.

If you would like to take this journey with the help of the Holy Spirit then let's begin. Let's travel towards Pentecost. This ancient feast is about setting aside a "week of weeks" plus one day to prepare for a spiritual harvest. Pentecost is actually the 50th day of Easter. As the early apostles gathered together for this feast, they experienced a new outpouring of the Holy Spirit, which also became the birth of the Church. Let God awaken you with his breath, and warm you with the fire of his love so that you too can celebrate a new birthday in the Spirit.

How to Use This Book

This prayer journal is a guidebook for building or rebuilding your spiritual life. It offers important Scriptural insights about faith in Jesus, vital images for the Holy Spirit, and insights about sacramental life from the *Catechism of the Catholic Church* (hereafter referred to as *CCC*, followed by the **section** number).

Who is it for? This journal is for anyone who would like to renew his or her relationship with the Holy Spirit. It is for people participating in a *New Life in the Spirit Seminar* (weekly topics are underlined in the summary). It is for adults who are preparing for Baptism and Confirmation, or for those who want follow-up for a weekend retreat. This journal is also appropriate for Advent, Lent, or the time from Easter to Pentecost. You can choose the number of weeks (and titles for the Spirit) that you would like to use on a daily retreat.

What's included? A **weekly opening section** focuses on one theme. It includes statements of faith, Scripture passages, and quotes from the *Catechism of the Catholic Church*, or parts of the Apostles' and Nicene **Creeds** (in bold print). Creeds are emphasized because they provide a summary of our faith. As St. Ambrose once said, the "Creed is the spiritual seal, our heart's meditation and an ever-present guardian; it is, unquestionably, the treasure of our soul." (*CCC*, 197). There is also a sprinkling of footnotes directing you to resources at the end of the journal. Each **numbered day** includes a meditation, a quote and the first lines of a prayer. **Day Three** for example, stands for the day of the current week that you are praying. The number in parenthesis, **(17)** for example, keeps track of the days if you are using the whole 50-day journal.

What if I miss a day? Don't worry about missing a day or about questions. These experiences are normal. Don't give up. As Saint Padre Pio said, "Go ahead! Courage! In the spiritual life he who does not go forward goes backward. It is the same with a (sail) boat that must always go forward. If it stands still the wind will blow it back." Remember, it is God who reaches out to us first. God is very interested in what you have to say. Make a commitment to use this journal for 15 minutes a day. Choose a specific time and place. God will help you keep your promise. If you are journaling alone, begin where you left off. If you are journaling with a group, prayerfully read all the missed entries at once and move forward with the group.

Where do I start? Read the **weekly opening section** each day, then the **numbered day**. Read the Scripture slowly and let it sink in. Read it twice. Underline any striking words. Read the journal prayer and finish it in your own words. Don't worry if you can't think of anything to underline or to write. There are no right words to say. Rest in God's presence. Then end with the following prayer.

Commitment Prayer

Jesus, I know now that I am Yours and You are mine
forever.
Thank You for sending Your Spirit to me
That I might have the power to live this new life with
You.
Stir up Your Spirit in me. Release Your Spirit in me.
Baptize me with the fullness of Your Spirit
That I may experience Your presence and
power in my life.
That I may find new meaning in your Scriptures.
That I may find new meaning in the sacraments.
That I may find delight and comfort in prayer.
That I may be able to love as you love and forgive
as You forgive.
That I may discover and use the gifts you give me for
the life of the Church.
That I may experience the peace and the joy that You
have promised us.
Fill me with Your Spirit, Jesus. I wish to receive all that
You have to give me.

Amen.

(1) Come, Holy Spirit, Lord and Giver of Life.

Summary   God is the source of all life and goodness. God's love is without limit or condition. There are signs of <u>God's love</u> in creation and even in our hearts.

Scripture   In the name of our Lord Jesus Christ, always give thanks for everything to God the Father. (Ephesians 5:20)

Church   **I believe in God, the Father almighty, creator of heaven and earth.**

Day One (1)

The same God who created all the galaxies and every microscopic being is with you now as you read these words. There is always more to discover about God and his infinite love. Watch and listen.

> When I look at the sky, which you have made,
> at the moon and the stars, which you set in their places
> —what are human beings, that you think of them;
> mere mortals, that you care for them?
> O LORD, our Lord, your greatness is seen in all the world!
> (Psalm 8:3-4,9)

Journal prayer: Come, Holy Spirit, give me eyes to see the Father. Give me a grateful heart even in the midst of turmoil. Even now I thank you for…

Day Two (2)

It is God who gave you life. God sustains you and wants to take care of your needs. So many times this love has been invisible and mysterious. So many times it has been clouded by sin and suffering. We don't always understand or see God.

> You created every part of me;
> you put me together in my mother's womb…
> When my bones were being formed…
> when I was growing there in secret,
> you knew that I was there – you saw me before I was born.
> (Psalm 139:13,15-16)

Journal prayer: I want to step back from my daily routine, God. I want to see your hand in my life. Show me how to recognize your presence especially when…

Day Three (3)

The Old Testament prophets use many images for God.
They compare God's care to the touch of a potter's hand or a
nursing mother. They describe God as a careful vinedresser
and a faithful husband. God is the "I Am Who Am," the God of
Abraham, and Yahweh. God is without end.[1]

> The LORD will comfort his people;
> he will have pity on his suffering people...
> "Even if a mother should forget her child,
> I will never forget you...
> I have written your name on the palms of my hands."
> (Isaiah 49:13,15-16)

Journal prayer: Who are you God? What name shall I give
you in my own heart? I have to start some place and I want to
lower the wall between you and me. For now I will call you...

Day Four (4)

The Apostle's Creed begins with a statement about God and about who we are as children of God. This statement is like a birth certificate, a declaration of our spiritual roots and origins. St. Paul realizes who we are when he prays on our behalf:

> I ask God from the wealth of his glory to give you power through his Spirit to be strong in your inner selves, and I pray that Christ will make his home in your hearts through faith. I pray that you may have your roots and foundation in love, so that you, together with all God's people, may have the power to understand how broad and long, how high and deep, is Christ's love. (Ephesians 3:16-18)

Journal prayer: You are the one who gave me life, God. You are at the center of my being. Help me find my spiritual roots and discover the many ways that you already love me. Help me see…

Day Five (5)

We have many dreams, plans, and desires that shape our search for happiness. But we usually have one big dream that wins out over all the others. What is it? What part does God's dream have in our plans? God's love gives us a blueprint from our maker, a vision for our happiness.

> "I alone know the plans I have for you, plans to bring you prosperity and not disaster, plans to bring about the future you hope for. Then you will call to me. You will come and pray to me, and I will answer you." (Jeremiah 29:11-12)

Journal prayer: Plans, maps, application forms and instructions can be hard to follow. But you, O Father, are the source of all strength. You have set me on a journey and given me a destination. Help me when I get lost, especially when…

Day Six (6)

God invites us into a covenant that is ratified and affirmed through the sacraments. God acts in our lives. God speaks to us. God touches us. God calls us back when we fail. God is love and offers us the fullness of life through a personal relationship with him.

> "Come, everyone who is thirsty – here is water!
> Come, you that have no money – buy grain and eat!...
> Come to me, and you will have life!
> I will make a lasting covenant with you." (Isaiah 55:1,3)

Journal prayer: I want so many things God. When I am in a mall there are so many things in front of me. When I have free time there are so many things to do. I want to learn how to choose you first. I want to belong to you and so I pray...

Day Seven (7)

We are made for a life of intimate union with the one God who is Father, Son and Holy Spirit. God has begun this new life in us through the sacraments of Baptism, Confirmation and Eucharist. The *Catechism* states:

> [Baptism is] *"the washing of regeneration and renewal by the Holy Spirit"* for it signifies and actually brings about the birth of water and the Spirit. (*CCC,* 1215)

> Holy Baptism is the basis of the whole Christian life, the gateway to life in the Spirit. (*CCC,* 1213)

> Confirmation brings an increase and deepening of baptismal grace… it gives us a special strength of the Holy Spirit to spread and defend the faith by word and action. (*CCC,* 1303)

Journal prayer: There is more to faith than I ever imagined. I want to start over again. Recreate me. Come, Holy Spirit and wash me clean. Open the gate for me. Come, Holy Spirit, give me…

(2) Come, Spirit of Truth and Hope. Come, Consoler Spirit, be my Help.

Summary   Through his life, death and resurrection Jesus becomes our <u>salvation</u>. "Belief in the true Incarnation of the Son of God is the distinctive sign of Christian faith." (*CCC*, 463)

Scripture   Jesus answered him, "I am the way, the truth, and the life." (John 14:6)

Church   **I believe in Jesus Christ, his only Son, our Lord.**

Through him all things were made. For us men and for our salvation he came down from heaven.

Day One (8)

The Scriptures outline a plan for human history, and according to that plan the Father wanted to be very close to us, so close that He sent Jesus to walk among us. Jesus became the centerpiece of salvation history and of God's personal, forgiving love for each of us.

> Christ is the visible likeness of the invisible God. He is the first-born Son, superior to all created things… God created the whole universe through him and for him. Christ existed before all things, and in union with him all things have their proper place. (Colossians 1:15-17)

Journal prayer: Come, Holy Spirit of wisdom. I need your help in order to recognize Jesus. Help me listen to Scripture. Help me remember what I have learned from the Church. Help me become more teachable as I…

Day Two (9)

Jesus is fully God and fully human. Through his life, death and resurrection Jesus heals the separation between God and us. He redeems us by taking on all the consequences of our sins. He restores our souls and carries us off into the Father's arms.

> [Jesus] of his own free will gave up all he had, and took the nature of a servant…
> He was humble and walked the path of obedience all the way to death – his death on the cross…
> And so, in honor of the name of Jesus all beings in heaven, on earth…
> will fall on their knees, and all will openly proclaim that Jesus Christ is Lord, to the glory of God the Father. (Philippians 2:7-8,10-11)

Journal prayer: Come, Holy Spirit. I fall on my knees before you. Give me the smallest kernel of faith so I can call out to Jesus and discover his love for me. My dream is…

Day Three (10)

Following Jesus is the goal of the Christian life. We hear this message in a song from *Godspell*, based on a prayer by St. Richard of Chichester. "Merciful Friend, Brother and Redeemer, may I know you more clearly, love you more dearly, and follow you more nearly, day by day."

> As Jesus walked along the shore of Lake Galilee, he saw two fishermen, Simon and his brother Andrew, catching fish with a net. Jesus said to them, "Come with me, and I will teach you to catch people." At once they left their nets and went with him. (Mark 1:16-18)

Journal prayer: Come, Holy Spirit of Truth. I know so little about Jesus. Give me a new passion for following him. Give me the grace to become more of a disciple, ready to listen when…

Day Four (11)

The Scriptures offer us many portraits of Jesus. It is good to explore these so that we can learn how to follow him. One kind of portrait is a Gospel story – like the healing of the woman with the hemorrhage in Luke 8:42-48. Another kind of portrait is made up of the many names for Jesus.

> Alpha and Omega, Bread of Life, Brother, King of Kings, Emmanuel, Shepherd, Healer, High Priest, Messiah, Lamb of God, Prince of Peace, Redeemer, Savior, Son of David, Son of Mary, Teacher, Son of God, Suffering Servant[2]

Journal prayer: *Read these names slowly, savoring each one in turn. Repeat the one or two that speak to your heart. You can alternate the name "Jesus" with the ones you have chosen.* Jesus, you are the _____. I know this when…

Day Five (12)

Jesus asks Peter a question in the "hinge passage" in Mark's Gospel. This question is the punch line and the climax in Mark. Jesus asks us the same question today. Let us pray for the strength to respond.

> [Jesus] asked them, "Tell me, who do people say I am?"
> "Some say that you are John the Baptist," they answered;
> "others say that you are Elijah… [or] one of the prophets."
> "What about you?" he asked them. "Who do you say I am?"
> Peter answered, "You are the Messiah." (Mark 8:27-29)

Journal prayer: *Use an ancient Eastern prayer as part of your response to this question*, "Lord Jesus Christ, Son of the living God, have mercy on me, a sinner." *Repeat it slowly for several minutes. Try to exhale and inhale with each successive phrase. Then tell Jesus your thoughts and feelings while praying this way.* Jesus I…

Day Six (13)

On Ash Wednesday the Church invites us to "Turn away from sin and be faithful to the Gospel." There are many times in our daily lives when we fail, and when we are faced with the failings of others. We can always return to God in prayer and through the Sacrament of Reconciliation.

> God is light, and there is no darkness at all in him... But if we live in the light – just as he is in the light – then we have fellowship with one another, and the blood of Jesus, his Son, purifies us from every sin. [But] if we say we have no sin, we deceive ourselves. (1 John 1:5,7-8)

Journal prayer: Jesus, give me new strength and hope. I choose you now, Jesus, as my Lord and Savior. I want to leave my sins and failings behind me. Help me as I...

☐ Yes!

Please send me a free copy of Charismatic Renewal Services' **Renewed Life** Catalog.

This full-color catalog contains lots of recommended books, music and videos on the Charismatic Renewal, plus many other fine Catholic materials to help you grow in the Spirit.

Name ✒

Additional line for name or address, if you need it. ✒

Address ✒

City ✒   State ✒   Zip Code ✒

Charismatic Renewal Services, Inc.
Renewed Life Catalog
4315 Ralph Jones Court
South Bend, IN 46628

Day Seven (14)

The *Catechism* reminds us: "through his grace, the Holy Spirit is the first to awaken faith in us and to communicate to us the new life, which is to 'know the Father and the one whom he has sent, Jesus Christ.'" (*CCC,* 684) We can be sure that the Spirit will help us find Jesus.

> St. Ambrose said: "When we speak about wisdom, we are speaking of Christ. When we speak about virtue, we are speaking about Christ. When we speak about justice, we are speaking of Christ. When we speak about peace, we are speaking of Christ. When we speak about truth and life and redemption, we are speaking of Christ."

Journal prayer: God, stir up your Spirit in me. Release your Spirit in me. Fill me with your Spirit that I might fall in love with Jesus in new ways. I wish to receive all that You have to give me, especially…

(3) Come, Holy Spirit, Living Water. You are the Spirit of Christ.

Summary   Like Jesus, we are called to live in the Holy Spirit
and continue the <u>new life</u> given through Baptism.

Scripture   "I have come in order that you might have life
—life in all its fullness." (John 10:10)

Church   **We believe in the Holy Spirit, the Lord, the
giver of life…**

Sacraments are "powers that come forth" from
the Body of Christ, which is ever-living and life-
giving. They are actions of the Holy Spirit.
(*CCC,* 1116)

Day One (15)

Even though Jesus was conceived by the power of Holy
Spirit,[3] and was sinless, he sought baptism in the Jordan. He
experienced a new manifestation of the Father's love and a
new outpouring of the Spirit. He experienced what St. Cyril of
Jerusalem called "a new kind of water."

> As soon as Jesus came up out of the water, he saw heaven
> opening and the Spirit coming down on him like a dove. And
> a voice came from heaven, "You are my own dear Son."
> (Mark 1:10-11)

Journal prayer: I use water everyday, God, but I still wake up
thirsty. Come, Holy Spirit. You are living water and I need a
new life, a new way of…

Day Two (16)

We are called to imitate Jesus in a vital, intimate relationship with the Holy Spirit. He had a conviction that the Spirit is real and active. People were astonished at his reading of Isaiah, and surprised when the promises behind the prophet's words took flesh through Jesus.

> "The Spirit of the Lord is upon me, because he has chosen me to bring good news to the poor... liberty to the captives and recovery of sight to the blind... and announce that the time has come when the Lord will save his people."
> (Luke 4:18-19)

Journal prayer: I listen to so many things in one day: music, conversations, television, and a multitude of sounds. But how do I listen for the voice of your Spirit? How can I consider every word that you speak? Open my ears, especially when I...

Day Three (17)

Jesus surrendered to the Father and to the Spirit. The ministry of Jesus was marked by the activity and the strength of the Spirit. The actions of Jesus were steeped in the gifts, fruits and charisms of the Spirit. And at his death the living water of the Spirit flowed from his side.

> You know about Jesus of Nazareth and how God poured out on him the Holy Spirit and power. He went everywhere, doing good and healing all who were under the power of the Devil, for God was with him. We are witnesses of everything that he did. (Acts 10:38-39)

Journal prayer: Some pictures of Jesus and the saints include a halo as a way of portraying the presence of the Holy Spirit. List one or two examples of the presence of the Spirit in something Jesus did. Think of a similar situation today. Ask Jesus to send his Spirit now.

Day Four (18)

We can imitate Jesus by seeking more of God's abundant life. Like Jesus, we can say "Yes" to more of the Holy Spirit. Jesus will help us. Following Jesus means choosing to live in the Holy Spirit, the Lord, the giver of life. We can only choose Jesus through the power of the Spirit.[4]

> Offer yourselves as a living sacrifice to God, dedicated to his service and pleasing to him… Let God transform you inwardly by a complete change of your mind. Then you will be able to know the will of God. (Romans 12:1-2)

Journal prayer: I want to give myself to you God, but I am not sure how pleasing my gift is. Come, Holy Spirit. Come, Living Water, wash me and make me holy. Change my…

Day Five (19)

The Baptism of Jesus is a very significant event. It brings a new anointing, a dynamic force that is evident in the life of Jesus as he resists evil and faces death. This anointing is unmistakable when Jesus surrenders his last breath and the centurion recognizes Jesus as the Son of God.

> The army officer who was standing there in front of the cross saw how Jesus had died, "This man was really the Son of God!" he said. (Mark 15:39)

Journal prayer: Jesus, you surrendered your whole life on the cross. The power of this surrender tore the curtains of the Temple and opened up graves. Open my heart. Open my grave. Unlock what I have kept closed to you. Come…

Day Six (20)

Baptism, Confirmation and Eucharist provide ongoing ways of choosing Jesus. We can draw daily strength from these sacraments. We can say "Yes" to the action of the Holy Spirit. We can say "No" to every kind of sin through the power of the Spirit.

> If the Spirit of God, who raised Jesus from death, lives in you, then he who raised Christ from death will also give life to your mortal bodies by the presence of his Spirit in you. (Romans 8:11)

Journal prayer: I choose to stand beside Jesus in the waters of the Jordan. I choose to live my own Baptism today, tomorrow and forever. I want to live in the Holy Spirit. Thank you for…

Day Seven (21)

St. Francis Cabrini once exclaimed, "Oh! If only devotion to the Holy Spirit inflamed the world, then should we see the face of the earth renewed, and Faith and Love would triumph." We are called to surrender to the Holy Spirit together for the sake of the whole world.

> In the same way the Spirit also comes to help us, weak as we are. For we do not know how we ought to pray; the Spirit himself pleads with God for us in groans that words cannot express. And God, who sees into our hearts, knows what the thought of the Spirit is; because the Spirit pleads with God on behalf of his people and in accordance with his will. (Romans 8:26-27)

Journal prayer: Oh God, you have promised me new power but I often feel helpless. Help me embrace your fire. Help me surrender with my sisters and brothers so we can build your Church in…

4) Come, Holy Spirit, Giver of Gifts, anoint us.

Summary Confirmation gives us "the full outpouring of the Holy Spirit as once granted to the apostles on the day of Pentecost." (*CCC,* 1302) Together Baptism, Confirmation and Eucharist help us <u>receive God's gifts</u>.

Scripture You have been purified from sin; you have been dedicated to God; you have been put right with God by the Lord Jesus Christ and by the Spirit of our God. (1 Corinthians 6:11)

Church **I believe in... the forgiveness of sins... and the life everlasting.**

Day One (22)

It is part of the human condition to want more. We want good things that last forever. We want to be outrageously happy: but Jesus presents us with a challenge and a paradox in how we achieve all these things.

> "If you want to come with me, you must forget yourself, take up your cross every day, and follow me. For if you want to save your own life, you will lose it, but if you lose your life for my sake, you will save it." (Luke 9:23-24)

Journal prayer: I want a new life, Jesus. I seek a new blossoming of your life. Help me die to self and sin on life's journey. Help me learn how to spend myself for others. Teach me new ways of…

Day Two (23)

At Confirmation we begin by renewing our Baptismal Vows. We reject sin and Satan. We ask Jesus for the strength of his Holy Spirit to overcome sin, and to reject false gods.

> "For those who ask will receive, and those who seek will find, and the door will be opened to anyone who knocks… As bad as you are, you know how to give good things to your children. How much more, then, will the Father in heaven give the Holy Spirit to those who ask him!" (Luke 11:10,13)

Journal prayer: When I look closely at my spiritual life I find half-hearted beliefs, patterns of sin and an inability to do good. Come, Holy Spirit, open the door to my heart. Forgive me for…

Day Three (24)

Jesus promised his disciples that he would send the Holy Spirit. This promise is for you. You can have an intimate relationship with the Holy Spirit as your teacher and helper.

> "I will ask the Father, and he will give you another Helper, who will stay with you forever. He is the Spirit, who reveals the truth about God… You know him, because he remains with you and is in you. When I go, you will not be left all alone." (John 14:16-18)

Journal prayer: Jesus, you had so many things to say when you knew that you were leaving. Your heart was overflowing with words of wisdom and hope. Speak to me too. *Skim through John 14 and find a few hopeful words. Write them in your own words. Imagine Jesus speaking them to you now.*

Day Four (25)

The *Catechism* describes Confirmation as a personal Pentecost. The celebration of this sacrament sets us on a journey of ongoing transformation. We are given new strength to live as disciples. We are not afraid of what lies ahead because of the power that lies within us.

> Confirmation… gives the Holy Spirit in order to… incorporate us more firmly into Christ, strengthen our bond with the Church… and help us bear witness to the Christian faith in words accompanied by deeds. (*CCC*, 1316)

Journal prayer: Holy Spirit, let the graces of this sacrament break forth in me. Give me an inner awareness of you. Awaken new faith in me. I think…

Day Five (26)

Was your celebration of Confirmation anything like Pentecost? Have you watched for the inner breeze of the Holy Spirit? Are you ready for someone to wake you up, to help you choose a life of ongoing conversion? Do you need someone to restore your soul?

> When the day of Pentecost came, all the believers were gathered together in one place. Suddenly there was a noise… like a strong wind blowing, and it filled the whole house… Then they saw what looked like tongues of fire which spread out and touched each person there. They were all filled with the Holy Spirit. (Acts 2:1-4)

Journal prayer: Come, Holy Spirit touch me from the top of my head to the bottom of my feet. Come, Holy Spirit, I place myself in the Upper Room with the Apostles. Show me…

Day Six (27)

When we receive the Sacrament of Confirmation[5] the predominant physical sign of the Spirit's presence is an anointing with oil, not the kind we use in salad or medicine but a holy oil that symbolizes God's indelible spiritual seal on our lives.

> Oil is a sign of abundance and joy; it cleanses (anointing before and after a bath) and limbers (the anointing of athletes and wrestlers); oil is a sign of healing, since it is soothing to bruises and wounds; and it makes radiant with beauty, health, and strength. (*CCC*, 1293)

Journal prayer: God, I need your touch and your cleansing. I need strength and healing. Jesus, stir up your Spirit in me. Release your Holy Spirit in me. Cover me with your presence and…

Day Seven (28)

In the Acts of the Apostles there are three outpourings of the Spirit: the Jerusalem Pentecost (2:1-42), one in Samaria (8:14-17), and the Gentile Pentecost (10:44-48). Jesus baptizes believers with fire over and over again. Pentecost repeats itself throughout the history of the Church.

> [St. John the Baptist said:] "I baptize you with water to show that you have repented, but the one who will come after me will baptize you with the Holy Spirit and fire." (Matthew 3:11)

Journal prayer: "Lord, I freely yield all my liberty to you. Take my memory, my intellect and my entire will. You have given me anything I am or have; I give it all back to you to stand under your will alone."[6] I pray for a new fire in…

(5) Come, Holy Spirit, Blessed Light and Living Flame of Love.

Summary   <u>Life in the Spirit</u> means receiving gifts, fruits and charisms of the Spirit.

Scripture   "I will pour out my Spirit on everyone: your sons and daughters will proclaim my message; your old people will have dreams." (Joel 2:28)

Church   Mary is the spouse of Holy Spirit and a companion as we seek a new Pentecost. She is a model for seeking the fullness of life in the Spirit.

Baptism in the Holy Spirit:

In the statement, *Grace for the New Springtime*, a national bishop's committee defines baptism in the Spirit as "a grace experience which touches every dimension of the Church's life…[and as] the reawakening in Christian experience of the presence and action of the Holy Spirit given in Christian initiation, and manifested in a broad range of charisms."[7]

People's experiences of baptism in the Spirit vary. Some are awakened suddenly and surrender to the Holy Spirit after a dramatic conversion experience. Some describe a gradual process, like waking up on a lazy Saturday morning. Some are immersed in the Spirit as they yield to a new thirst for reading Scripture, others, during a time of private prayer. One man wanted to worship God while driving to work but couldn't remember the words of any hymns. As he gave himself to God he began to pray in tongues. Many are awakened to the life of the Spirit through Holy Spirit seminars[8], faith-sharing groups and the gesture called the "laying on of hands." Most of us need the support of a small community in order to break patterns of amnesia about what God wants to do.

God has a timetable and beginning experiences that are just right for each of us. Trust God to unleash the Holy Spirit in your life. Seek out the help of other believers and ask them to pray with you often. It may also be helpful to know how God has been calling other Catholics in the United States to charismatic discipleship[9] or to order a free copy of *Pentecost Today,* a newsletter that fosters baptism in the Spirit as a normal part of our faith experience. (See the back page.) And if you haven't received all the Sacraments of Initiation find someone who can help you make connections with the local Church.

The Church affirms our need for new beginnings in the Holy Spirit in a variety of ways: through the annual celebration of Pentecost, through the renewal of baptismal vows during the Easter Season, through the prominence of baptismal fonts and holy water so we can repeat the Sign of the Cross, and finally through the Profession of the Nicene Creed at celebrations of the Eucharist.

If you would like a new outpouring of the Holy Spirit, there are steps you can take. First, review what you have written in this journal and thank God for what is happening. Second, carefully consider your Baptismal Vows. The Holy Spirit gives us the strength to **believe** in God, which literally means to "fall in love." John reminds us that, "It is not that we have loved God, but that he loved us and sent his Son." (1 John 4:10) Ask yourself each question out loud and respond with your heart.

Renewal of Baptismal Vows

Do you reject sin, so as to live in the freedom of God's children? *Response.*
Do you reject Satan, father of sin and prince of darkness? *Response.*

Do you believe in God, the Father almighty, creator of heaven and earth? ***Response.***

Do you believe in Jesus Christ, his only Son, our Lord, who was born of the Virgin Mary, was crucified, died and was buried, rose from the dead, and is now seated at the right hand of the Father? ***Response.***

Do you believe in the Holy Spirit, the holy Catholic Church, the communion of saints, the forgiveness of sins, and the resurrection of the body and life everlasting? ***Response.***

Day One (29)

Our own willingness and ability to receive the Holy Spirit is a function of the images we have for the Holy Spirit, and a desire to experience God's Spirit as a person. Consider these images that come from Scripture, the saints and the Church's Pentecost prayer.

> Spirit of Truth, Paraclete, Invisible One, Breath of God, Wind, Living Flame, Dove, Mighty Wind, Soul of Church, Comforter, Light, Consoler Spirit, Seat of Wisdom, Soul's Welcome Guest, Spirit of Truth, Spirit of Christ, Seal, Advocate, Giver of Life, Still Point.[10]

Journal prayer: Come, Holy Spirit enlighten my senses and my mind. Show me who you want to be in my life. I choose to call you… (*Relax and repeat one or two titles slowly for a few minutes. Imagine the Spirit lifting you up and presenting you to Jesus.*)

Day Two (30)

Mary was no stranger to the workings of the Holy Spirit. Her first "Yes" to the Spirit brought God's greatest gift of all, the incarnation of Jesus. She is a model for surrender as she prays with the disciples in the Upper Room.

> The angel answered, "The Holy Spirit will come on you, and God's power will rest upon you. For this reason the holy child will be called the Son of God... For there is nothing that God cannot do." (Luke 1:35-37)

Journal prayer: Mary, please ask the Holy Spirit to come to me. Pray with me so that I might receive the fullness of the Holy Spirit. Help me be an instrument of God's love for...

Day Three (31)

A Russian bishop named St. Dimitrii of Rostov prayed, "Come, my Light, and illumine my darkness. Come, my Life, and revive me from death… Come, Flame of Divine Love, and burn up the thorns of my sins, kindling my heart with the flame of your love."

> Even gold, which can be destroyed, is tested by fire; and so your faith, which is much more precious than gold, must also be tested, so that it may endure… So you rejoice with a great and glorious joy which words cannot express, because you are receiving the salvation of your souls. (1 Peter 1:7-9)

Journal prayer: Come, Holy Spirit. I want to be an instrument of your praise and thanksgiving. I want to join the saints and the angels in giving you glory. I thank you for… I praise you for…

Day Four (32)

The coming of each new day is governed by the rising of the sun. In the same way, every day provides a new opportunity to choose the light of God's Spirit and to reject the darkness by walking with Jesus. God's Living Flame will guide us.

> You yourselves used to be in the darkness, but since you have become the Lord's people, you are in the light. So you must live like people who belong to the light, for it is the light that brings a rich harvest of every kind of goodness, righteousness and truth. (Ephesians 5:8-9)

Journal prayer: Come, Living Flame of Love. Come into the darkest moments of my day and remind me of the presence of Jesus. Come, Living Flame of Love. I chose…

Day Five (33)

When seeking more of the life in the Spirit it is important to resist the urge to focus on your experiences and feelings. Positive or negative feelings are not the most reliable barometer for what God is doing. Trust God's love for you. Focus on thanking Jesus for the gifts being given.

> The seven *gifts* of the Holy Spirit are wisdom, understanding, counsel, fortitude, knowledge, piety, and fear of the Lord. They belong in their fullness to Christ, Son of David. They complete and perfect the virtues of those who receive them. (*CCC*, 1831)

Journal prayer: I know how often I have failed in cooperating with any one of these gifts, Jesus. Please forgive me and help me start over. Come, Holy Spirit, as I continue to pray for the gift of…

Day Six (34)

A person who lives in the Spirit will also bear the fruit of the Spirit. The *Catechism* reminds us that these fruits and growth in holiness are the proof of God's presence. (*CCC,* 1832)

> The Spirit produces love, joy, peace, patience, kindness, goodness, faithfulness, humility, and self-control. There is no law against such things as these… The Spirit has given us life; he must also control our lives. (Galatians 5:22-23,25)

Journal prayer: I feel like I am only taking baby steps in following you, Jesus. I feel like I have so much to learn about being an instrument of your love. Increase the fruit of …

Day Seven (35)

Not many people are taught to expect charisms during their preparation for sacraments; but charisms are meant to be a normal part of the Christian life and are meant to direct our attention to God. Openness to charisms is a very important way to respond to the Holy Spirit.

In Scripture there are several lists of charisms that include: administration, celibacy, craftsmanship, discernment, evangelism, encouragement, faith, giving, healing, intercession, interpretation of tongues, knowledge, leadership, mercy, inspired music, prophecy, teaching, praying in tongues[11], voluntary poverty, and wisdom.

> Charisms are to be accepted with gratitude by the person who receives them and by all members of the Church as well. They are a wonderfully rich grace for the apostolic vitality and for the holiness of the entire Body of Christ, provided they are really genuine gifts of the Holy Spirit. (*CCC,* 800).

Journal prayer: Holy Spirit, I choose the gifts and charisms that you want for me. I pray that I may discover and use the gifts you give me for the life of the Church. Fill me with Your Spirit, Jesus. I wish to receive all that you have to give me and so I pray…

(6) Come, Holy Spirit, Soul of the Church, Seat of Wisdom.

Summary   The Holy Spirit calls us together in Jesus. The Spirit <u>helps us grow</u> to spiritual maturity through sacraments, prayer, Scripture, study, community and service.

Scripture   "I am the vine, and you are the branches. Those who remain in me, and I in them, will bear much fruit; for you can do nothing without me." (John 15:5)

Church   **I believe in… the holy catholic Church, [and] the communion of saints**.

Day One (36)

The Scriptures offer images for Church[12] community: the vine and the branches, the family of God, the parts of a body, being in a boat together, the temple, the new Jerusalem and the disciples' relationships with Jesus. At the heart of all of these images is the presence and work of the Spirit.

> Come to the Lord, the living stone rejected by people as worthless but chosen by God as valuable. Come as living stones, and let yourselves be used in building the spiritual temple. (1 Peter 2:4-5)

Journal prayer: Come, Holy Spirit, Soul of the Church. I need a spiritual home. I need to be part of something much bigger than myself in order to thrive and grow. I need your…

Day Two (37)

One way we live in the Spirit is by encountering Jesus through the sacraments. God has given us seven sacraments that address every human hunger: Baptism, Confirmation, Eucharist, Reconciliation, Matrimony, the Anointing of the Sick, and Holy Orders.

> "I am the bread of life," Jesus told them. "Those who come to me will never be hungry; those who believe in me will never be thirsty... I am the living bread that came down from heaven. If you eat this bread, you will live forever." (John 6:35,51)

Journal prayer: Close your eyes and picture yourself inside a church building. Look around at the windows, the altar, the statues... Tell God how you feel about being there. Picture Jesus coming toward you. Let him embrace you and respond to your needs. Write down his words to you.

Day Three (38)

One way we live in the Spirit is by choosing a life of daily prayer.[13] Jesus prayed often: before choosing the apostles, and before raising Lazarus. He prayed on Mount Tabor and on the Mount of Olives.

> News about Jesus spread all the more widely, and crowds of people came to hear him and be healed from their diseases. But he would go away to lonely places, where he prayed. (Luke 5:15-16)

Journal prayer: Come, O Seat of Wisdom, and help me find the time and the desire to pray. Help me reorganize my life and face the many obstacles to spending time with you, especially…

Day Four (39)

We grow in the Spirit through studying the Scriptures[14] and the teaching of the Church.[15] St. Augustine exhorts us to grow as we "fix the eye of faith on the divine word of the Holy Scripture as on a light shining in a dark place until the day dawn and the day-star arise in our hearts."

> Jesus explained to them what was said about himself in all the Scriptures, beginning with the books of Moses and the writings of all the prophets… Then their eyes were opened and they recognized him… They said to each other, "Wasn't it like a fire burning in us when he talked to us on the road and explained the Scriptures to us?" (Luke 24:27,31-32)

Journal prayer: Come Holy Spirit, I choose you as my teacher. I choose to learn more about following Jesus. Help me find the resources that I need to grow in faith. Give me new ways of…

Day Five (40)

Life in the Spirit means growth and maturity within the community of God's people (in a garden instead of a single pot). It means choosing a specific faith community. It means faith sharing, prayer and learning in small sharing groups, in prayer groups, in large gatherings, or in liturgical settings.

> [Christ chose some] to be apostles, others to be prophets, others to be evangelists... He did this to prepare all God's people for the work of Christian service, in order to build up the body of Christ... We shall become mature people, reaching to the very height of Christ's full stature.
> (Ephesians 4:11-13)

Journal prayer: I choose to grow in the garden of your Church, Lord. I choose love and forgiveness as a way of life. Help me find ways to belong to your people and grow in...

Day Six (41)

Life in the Spirit means embracing a life of service. It means finding deliberate ways to imitate the compassion of Jesus. It means using charisms as tools for loving the hungry, the lost, the poor, the ignorant, prisoners, and the homeless in our families, parishes and local communities.

> You should each give, then, as you have decided, not with regret or out of a sense of duty; for God loves the one who gives gladly… And God, who supplies seed for the sower and bread to eat, will also supply you with all the seed you need and will make it grow and produce a rich harvest from your generosity. (2 Corinthians 9:7,10)

Journal prayer: Come, Holy Spirit. Touch my heart. Make me a sign of your love and an instrument of your presence to the world around me. Help me serve those who…

Day Seven (42)

Life in the Spirit involves a plan that includes regular prayer, study, community and service. When we grow weary we can imitate the example of the saints. "The Spirit is truly the dwelling of the saints… since they offer themselves as a dwelling place for God." (*CCC*, 2684)

> As for us, we have this large crowd of witnesses around us. So then, let us rid ourselves of… sin which holds onto us so tightly, and let us run with determination the race that lies before us. Let us keep our eyes fixed on Jesus, on whom our faith depends from beginning to end. (Hebrews 12:1-2)

Journal prayer: Come, Holy Spirit. Lift me up when I get the breath knocked out of me. Help me persevere in becoming a saint in your Church. I rely on your presence and not on my own efforts to…

(7) Come, Holy Spirit, Sanctifier and Breath of God.

Summary   In addition to the call to maturity (growth), and the call to community, God invites us to a life of holiness (spiritual <u>transformation</u>) and to mission.

Scripture   "'Our Father in heaven: May your holy name be honored; may your Kingdom come; may your will be done on earth as it is in heaven.'" (Matthew 6:9-10)

Church   The Christian "is called by God to burn with the spirit of Christ and to exercise his [or her] apostolate in the world as a kind of leaven." (*Decree on the Apostolate of Lay People*, 2.)

Day One (43)

As we are drawn into the life of the Father, Son and Holy Spirit, we undergo inner transformation. We want to please God. God becomes a wellspring for all that we are and do as we become holy.

> For it is by God's grace that you have been saved through faith. It is not the result of your own efforts, but God's gift… In our union with Christ Jesus he has created us for a life of good deeds, which he has already prepared for us to do. (Ephesians 2:8-10)

Journal prayer: Come, Holy Spirit breathe your life into everything that I do, into every relationship that I enjoy, and into every place I enter. I choose your holiness from this day forward. Help me …

Day Two (44)

It takes time to grow into a life that gives glory to Jesus. We are apprentices in seeking, developing, and using gifts and charisms. We can depend on God's guidance along the way.

> Clothe yourselves with compassion, kindness, humility, gentleness, and patience.... And to all of these qualities add love, which binds all things together in perfect unity... Christ's message in all of its richness must live in your hearts. (Colossians 3:12,14,16)

Journal prayer: Come, Holy Spirit, blessed Sanctifier, take down the walls around my heart. Make me an instrument of your good pleasure and a willing apprentice in faith. I surrender to…

Day Three (45)

Holiness involves a paradox. It involves our ongoing consent and a great deal of letting go. We are called to a radical conversion of mind, heart, attitude and behavior. St. Therese of Lisieux once said, "You cannot be half a saint. You must be a whole saint or no saint at all."

> May the God who gives us peace make you holy in every way and keep your whole being – spirit, soul, and body – free from every fault at the coming of our Lord Jesus Christ. He who calls you will do it, because he is faithful.
> (1 Thessalonians 5:23-24)

Journal prayer: I choose the changes that come with loving you, Jesus. I choose to live for you alone. I want to be a saint and I will start by…

Day Four (46)

Together we must reflect the love of Jesus, and the workings of the Holy Spirit who is the primary agent of the Church's mission.[16] Jesus sends us into the world, as Church, to make disciples and to serve.

> "The Kingdom of heaven is like this. A woman takes some yeast and mixes it with a bushel of flour until the whole batch of dough rises." (Matthew 13:33)

Journal prayer: Show me how to use the charisms and gifts that you give me for your Kingdom. Jesus, let me be moved by your Spirit and filled with your gifts, especially the gift of...

Day Five (47)

Gifts and charisms are for the building of the Church and for serving the needs of the world.[17] These tools are for use in daily life and in the context of the Church's many-faceted evangelizing ministries.

> "You are like salt for the whole human race…. You are like light for the whole world. A city built on a hill cannot be hid… Your light must shine before people, so that they will see the good things you do and praise your Father in heaven." (Matthew 5:13-14,16)

Journal prayer: *Pray with a globe, a map, or a newspaper. Offer different countries to God*, "Holy Father I give you the people of… Send them your Spirit. Breathe on them and make them your own." *Praying in tongues is also an appropriate way to intercede. Conclude with*, "Make me an instrument of your presence in my daily life, in my parish, and in the world."

Day Six (48)

God will give you a place in the mission of the Church. Persevere in keeping a journal. Review it often to discover enduring invitations from God. Share what you hear in your faith community.

> They were worried and helpless, like sheep without a shepherd. So he said to his disciples, "The harvest is large, but there are few workers to gather it in. Pray to the owner of the harvest that he will send out workers to gather in his harvest." (Matthew 9:36-38)

Journal prayer: "God of love and mercy, you call us to be your people, you gift us with your abundant grace. Make us a holy people, radiating the fullness of your love. Form us into a community, a people who care, expressing your compassion. Remind us day after day of our baptismal call to serve, with joy and courage… Through Jesus and in your Spirit, we make this prayer."[18]

Day Seven (49)

We are always on the eve of yet another baptism in the Holy Spirit, until the day when each of us will be carried into a church and clothed with a baptismal robe for one last time. On that day we are ushered into an eternal immersion in the life of the Father, Son and Holy Spirit. Alleluia!

> "Do not be afraid, little flock, for your Father is pleased to give you the Kingdom." (Luke 12:32)
> "For only a penny you can buy two sparrows, yet not one sparrow falls to the ground without your Father's consent.... So do not be afraid; you are worth much more than many sparrows!" (Matthew 10:29,31)

Journal prayer: Jesus, I thank you for all that you have done to bring me closer to you. I trust you to lead me forward. I know that you will stay with me forever and so I pray...

Come Holy Spirit. Come Paraclete. Make the world your temple.

Day Fifty (50)

As Catholic Christians we have inherited many treasures from the Hebrew people. One of the most important riches is the idea that we don't just recall the events of Scripture, we relive them. Let's look at the account of Pentecost and its details in this light.

Pentecost begins with a communal release of the Holy Spirit. It is a very dramatic event with a wind that reminds us of God's creative Spirit at the beginning of the world (see Psalm 33:6). The tongues of fire remind us of the burning bush on Mt. Sinai (see Exodus 3:1-6) and God's covenant with his people (see Exodus 24:12-18). And the most remarkable phenomenon is the new zeal of the disciples. Peter emerges to proclaim the Good News about Jesus. He knows the Holy Spirit as a Paraclete (an advocate standing by his side). He "speaks plainly" about the resurrection of his Savior.

We are also called to be like Peter and the early disciples in their willingness to proclaim Jesus. We are called to evangelize, to bring the gospel into every human situation. The Holy Spirit will empower us in a wide variety of ways. The United States bishops have explained this call to evangelize in a document called **Go and Make Disciples:** *A National Plan and Strategy for Catholic Evangelization in the United States.*[19] There are three different kinds of evangelization. The first is to live our faith with an openness to lovingly share it with others. The second is to offer a gentle invitation to a personal relationship with Jesus and the Church. The third is to transform the world around us until Gospel values become the heartbeat of every human endeavor and the earth becomes God's temple.

> Many miracles and wonders were being performed among the people by the apostles... More and more people were added to the group – a crowd of men and women who believed in the Lord. (Acts 5:12,14)

Journal prayer: "Come, true light. Come, eternal life. Come, hidden mystery... Come, light without sunset. Come, infallible hope of all who must be saved. Come, awakener of all who sleep. Come, resurrection of the dead... Come, eternal joy. Come, incorruptible crown... Come, my breath and my life. Come, consolation of my poor soul. Come, my joy, my glory, my delight forever."[20] Then send me where you will, Lord.

Treasury of Prayers

St. Therese of Lisieux says, "For me, prayer is a surge of the heart; it is a simple look turned toward heaven, it is a cry of recognition and of love, embracing both trial and joy. It is a vast supernatural force which opens out my heart and binds me close to Jesus."

Our Father

Our Father, who art in heaven, hallowed be your name. Your kingdom come. Your will be done on earth, as it is in heaven. Give us this day our daily bread, and forgive us our trespasses, as we forgive those who trespass against us, and lead us not into temptation, but deliver us from evil. [For the kingdom, the power and the glory are yours, now and forever.] Amen.

Glory Be

Glory be to the Father, and to the Son, and to the Holy Spirit, as it was in the beginning, is now and ever shall be, world without end. Amen.

Come, Holy Spirit

Come, Holy Spirit, fill the hearts of your faithful, and enkindle in them the fire of your love. Send forth your Spirit, and we will be created, and you shall renew the face of the earth. O God, who by the light of the Holy Spirit, instructed the hearts of the faithful, grant that by that same Spirit, we may be truly wise, and ever rejoice in his consolation, through Christ our Lord, Amen.

Apostles' Creed

I believe in God, the Father almighty, creator of heaven and earth. I believe in Jesus Christ, his only Son, our Lord. He was conceived by the power of the Holy Spirit and born of the Virgin Mary. He suffered under Pontius Pilate, was crucified, died, and was buried. He descended into hell. On the third day he rose again. He ascended into heaven and is seated at the right hand of the Father. He will come again to judge the living and the dead. I believe in the Holy Spirit, the holy catholic church, the communion of saints, the forgiveness of sins, the resurrection of the body, and life everlasting. Amen.

St. Augustine's Prayer

Breathe in me, O Holy Spirit, that my thoughts may all be holy. Act in me, O Holy Spirit, that my work, too, may be holy. Strengthen me, O Holy Spirit, that I may defend all that is holy. Guard me, O Holy Spirit, that I may always be holy.

Endnotes, Books and Resources

[1] For more about belief in the Father see *CCC,* 268-274, 315-324. The *Catechism of the Catholic Church* is available online at www.vatican.va/archive/catechism_toc.htm or at www.usccb.org/catechism/text/instructions.htm You can also search for subjects in the *Catechism* at www.kofc.org/faith/catechism/catechism.cfm.

[2] For more about Jesus see *CCC,* 430-455 and 619-623.

[3] For more about the Holy Spirit see *CCC,* 683-701.

[4] To learn more read *The Holy Spirit in the Life of Jesus* by Raniero Cantalamessa (Collegeville, MN: The Liturgical Press, 1994). A comprehensive look at the way Jesus cooperated with the Spirit. To learn more about baptism in the Spirit in the early Church read *Fanning the Flame: What Does Baptism in the Holy Spirit Have to Do with Christian Initiation?* Edited by Kilian McDonnell and George Montague (Collegeville, MN:The Liturgical Press, 1991).

[5] For more about Confirmation see *CCC,* 1290-1296, 1302-1305.

[6] St. Ignatius of Loyola.

[7] *Grace for the New Springtime*, NCCB Ad Hoc Committee for Catholic Charismatic Renewal, March 1997.

[8] *Introduction to the Catholic Charismatic Renewal* by John and Therese Boucher (Ann Arbor, MI: Servant Publications, 1994). A booklet that describes the charismatic renewal.

[9] For a history of renewal read *As By a New Pentecost: The Dramatic Beginnings of the Catholic Charismatic Renewal* by Patti Gallagher Mansfield (Steubenville, OH: Franciscan University Press, 1992). For explanations of elements of the renewal see the *Dove Pamphlet Pack* available through *Renewed Life* at 800-348-2227.

[10] For images of the Spirit see *CCC,* 691-701. For a book about the Holy Spirit read *The Sanctifier,* translation of *El Espiritu Santo* by Luis M. Martinez, late Archbishop of Mexico (Boston, MA: Pauline Books and Media, 1985).

[11] Praying in tongues is "'a common gift of prayer by which we can

surrender our voice and thoughts to God, what Father Montague describes as a 'spirit-language' that gives voice to our inner self before God... [it] can be a gateway to the charismatic dimensions of faith. It gives a person a clear experience of being fully active in prayer, yet touched by the presence of the Holy Spirit.'" ("Charisms and the *New Life in the Spirit Seminars*," *Pentecost Today,* July/August/September 2001 p 12.)

[12] For more about the Church see *CCC*, 748-810.

[13] For online daily prayer visit *Sacred Space* at http://www.jesuit.ie/prayer/. For more about a developed spiritual life read *Following Jesus: A Disciple's Guide to Discerning God's Will* by John Boucher (Pecos, NM: Dove Publications, 1995).

[14] For a practical book about the meaning of the Bible see *Reading Scripture as the Word of God* by George Martin (Ann Arbor, MI: Servant Publications, 1997).

[15] For a catalogue of resources that includes Catholic and charismatic materials ask for a seasonal copy of *Renewed Life* at 800-348-2227.

[16] *Called and Gifted for the Third Millennium* (November 1995). United States Catholic Conference, Inc. www.nccbuscc.org/laity/calleden.htm. Booklet offering a vision of lay ministry and good descriptions of the call to holiness, community, mission and maturity.

[17] For an important article about using charisms in ministry read "Gifts for the church or gifts for the kingdom?" by George Montague, SM. (*Pentecost Today*, January/February/March 2001, p 9)

[18] From *Called and Gifted for the Third Millennium*, p v.

[19] **Go and Make Disciples:** *A National Plan and Strategy for Catholic Evangelization in the United States. U.S. Catholic Bishops (November 1992). Text, Study Guide and Implementation Process by Susan W. Blum, Ed. D.* (Washington, DC: National Council for Catholic Evangelization, 1994). Special study guide with faith-sharing questions and planning process available at: *http://www.catholicevangelization. org/products.*

[20] Simeon the New Theologian, Hymns, 949-1022.